COLLECTOR'S GUIDE TO

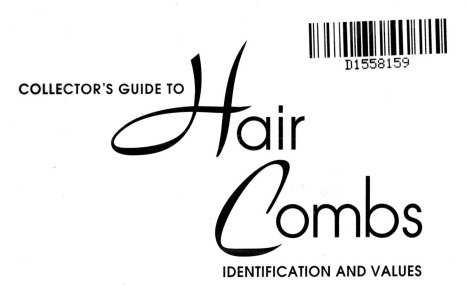

# Hair Combs

## IDENTIFICATION AND VALUES

by
Mary Bachman

Southern
Oregon
Antiques &
Collectibles
Club

COLLECTOR BOOKS

The current values of this book should be used only as a guide. They are not intended to set prices, which vary from one section of the country to another. Auction prices as well as dealer prices vary and are affected by condition as well as demand. Neither the Author nor the Publisher assumes responsibility for any losses that might be incurred as a result of consulting this guide.

# Searching for a Publisher?

We are always looking for knowledgeable people considered to be experts within their fields. If you feel that there is a real need for a book on your collectible subject and have a large comprehensive collection, contact Collector Books.

## On the Cover:

Clockwise from top right corner:
Sterling, with three oak leaves, 4¼"w x 5"h, $50.00 – 60.00.
Brass hair ornament, 2½"w x 4½"h, $45.00 – 55.00.
Wooden comb from Ghana, Africa, $125.00.
French jet, circa 1880 – 1890, 3¼"w x 6"h, $55.00 – 75.00.
Faux tortoise with aluminum top, sets, circa 1890, 4½"w x 5½"h, $80.00 – 90.00.
Horn with sterling top, lily of the valley design, Art Nouveau, $75.00 – 100.00.

Back photo:
Horned comb, clarified, dyed to look like tortoise shell, early 1800s, $55.00 – 75.00.

Cover design by Beth Summers
Book design by Holly C. Long
Photography by Mary Bachman

Additional copies of this book may be ordered from:
Collector Books
P.O. Box 3009
Paducah, Kentucky 42002 – 3009

@$16.95. Add $2.00 for postage and handling.
Copyright © 1998 by Mary Bachman

# Contents

# Introduction

This book is mostly about sharing my collection with other people who are interested in the beautiful combs our ancestors used to decorate their hair. Most of my combs were made from the early 1700s to approximately 1930. Some collectors are lucky enough to have found much older combs than this, but most combs of antiquity are in museums, where it is possible to see combs as old as from the Bronze Age. Besides bronze, these combs were made from natural materials such as ivory and bone, and even some wooden combs have survived the ages.

Since my background is in the arts, the comb designs were interesting to me. When I started to collect combs in 1986, celluloid was the predominate material that I saw, and it also was inexpensive. Little did I know that as my interest grew so would the prices I was willing to pay. The variety of colors and designs were intriguing, so the search was on to get a sample of each. I soon was collecting other materials as well, as I became aware that they existed. Horn, ivory, silver, brass, vulcanized rubber, and tortoise shell opened up the field of collecting combs for me. My collection at this time is approximately 300, which is small compared to some collectors. However, I have been selective in my collection, and I think it is a fairly good one. I haven't been fortunate in finding very many ivory combs, so I am constantly on the look out for any kind of ivory, especially the beautifully carved Oriental combs.

As one collects an item they enjoy, there are always questions that just have to be answered. How did women wear combs? How were they made? How old are they? How do you know what the material is? How do you test it? How do you preserve your collection? Collecting can become an obsession. This is the reason I wanted to put my combs into a book, for my own benefit as well as others.

The information I have

4

given is to the best of my knowledge. Dating combs is the most difficult aspect of collecting. Many collectors disagree on just when a certain comb was mostly likely made. I have not given a date for many of my combs because of this uncertainty. Periods that a certain kind of comb were worn overlapped into others. Materials were used over long periods of time. Combs were seldom dated. We have only an occasional trademark and our knowledge of different periods in history to help us in this endeavor. Even some experts will differ in their judgment of dates, but with experience we have a pretty good idea of when many of our combs were made and worn.

I have given what I feel are fair prices. Prices vary across the country, but with experience, collectors will know when they are getting a bargain or paying too much. There is always a piece that is rare with a price that is more than you would like to pay, but because it is rare you give in. If you don't, you usually regret it later on. There are still some materials that I haven't been able to find, such as gutta percha, Whitney jet, and Berlin iron. So that is what keeps me looking and hoping I'll still find some of the more unusual combs.

# Celluloid

Celluloid was a great discovery when developed in 1869 by John Hyatt. At the time he was looking for a replacement for ivory that was used to make billiard balls. Ivory was becoming harder to get and was very expensive. Celluloid, on the other hand, turned out to be much less expensive. Nitrocellulose and camphor were the main ingredients of celluloid. Cellulose was bought in large rolls of tissue paper which were shredded, washed, and dried. In the nitrating process they put the cellulose in a bath of nitric and sulfuric acids. It was then spun in a wire basket to remove the acids. Repeated washing and drying were necessary to cleanse the cellulose. At this point, camphor, a product from the bark of a camphor laurel tree, was introduced as a solvent. The large soft mass that resulted could then be rolled out into sheets. It was rolled many times until it became uniform in appearance. Only when celluloid was heated was it in a "plastic" state. When it cooled it became solid. The sheets were put in heated sheds to season for several weeks. When it came out it was usually in a warped condition

so that it had to be flattened and polished. In the beginning, celluloid was thought of as a substitute for natural materials such as horn, tortoise shell, and ivory, so their efforts were all put into making celluloid look like something it wasn't.

Celluloid was colorless in its beginning stages and accepted colorants easily. One can find almost every color in celluloid when collecting combs. If they were going to make imitation tortoise shell, they would put amber colored celluloid through the rollers while placing bits of dark brown celluloid into it. They kept rolling it until the pattern became uniform and took on the look of tortoise shell. Another method of creating the appearance of tortoise shell was by painting stripes and mottling on the celluloid by hand with an aniline brown solution mixed with a little fuchsin.

Tortoise shell was not the only thing that celluloid imitated. By stacking thin sheets of celluloid in various shades of cream together, with heat and a great deal of pressure, they would fuse. By cutting across the grain in the sheeting machine they came up with a wonderful imitation ivory. This material was used for many things besides combs. You can seldom go to an antique store that you don't see part of a dresser set that may contain everything from a comb, brush, and mirror to matching hair receivers, nail buffers, powder dishes, picture frames, and various other pieces to put on a lady's vanity. Ladies of the United States associated good fashion with Paris, so some manufacturers promoted their goods by calling them "Parisian Ivory." Because manufacturers were so good at imitating these materials it has been necessary to test combs to know if they are celluloid, tortoise shell, ivory, or horn. One way is to shave a little material from the side of a tooth on to a plate. Push the fine shavings close together and hold a match close to it. If it is celluloid it will either flash or flame up, and leave no residue. Horn, when burned, will smell of burnt hair. If the material is tortoise shell there will be no flame up in the fire test, and there should be some residue.

Celluloid combs, being cheaper to make, made the decorative comb more available so every lady was able to own these lovely hair adornments. It is interesting to see old 1895 Montgomery Ward catalogs with prices for these combs under 50 cents. Today a simple celluloid comb may cost from a few dollars to $30 or $40, while one with an elaborate design can be as much as $200 or more.

At first celluloid was quite plain with little embellishment. One later innovation was fusing a color over clear celluloid. Black was the most frequently used. I have found no reference to a so-called "watermarked" comb but I have a few combs that have that appearance. Pearlized was a similar surface that is still seen used in toilet seats, etc. They made imitation jewels of glass which were faceted and often backed with foil to give them extra sparkle. The imitation jewels of glass are referred to as pastes, brilliant sets, or rhinestones. They discovered they could embed sets into the plastic. When they clustered the sets so close together that you couldn't see between them they called it pavé or paved. Gold and silver were sometimes inlayed in a method called "pique d'or," which was used earlier on tortoise shell. These combs are usually imprinted on the back with the information that tells you its either 18K or 22K gold inlay. Another form of decoration was "niello." Brass was incised in a pattern and the design was filled with a black alloy which could be silver, copper, lead, or the like having a deep black color. The brass was

then fastened to the top of a
celluloid comb. Brass was also
cast into beetles, flowers, and
other shapes and fastened to a
comb. French jet, which is
faceted black glass, was used to
decorate as well. It was cut in
many different shapes and
sometimes fastened to wire,
giving it a light, delicate
appearance. Filigree was used
often on back combs. A fine
wire was fastened to the top of
a comb to form a scroll pattern
or outline a pattern of sets. The
designers of the day were constantly creating new patterns
and it is unusual for a collector
to find two identical combs.
The variations seem endless.

As wonderful as celluloid
was it had its drawbacks. During the manufacturing of the
plastic if there was even a
small spark there could be a
flash fire, so there were many
accidents, a few fatal. They
developed a water system that
was on the roof that could be
quickly dispensed to squelch a
fire. It has been told that some
workers wore their bathing
suits because there was so
much water needed to keep
sparks from occurring. Mean-
while there was a constant
search for formulas that were
less flammable. Several plastics were developed by other
companies and they found their
place in the comb industry.

Celluloid is susceptible to
breaking down. Collectors call

this the "virus." A comb will
first develop a light patch that
will soon begin to craze. Later
it will crumble and you've just
lost a lovely comb and your
investment. We have been told
to remove any damaged combs
so that other combs near by
won't catch the virus. Preserva-
tionists are constantly search-
ing for methods to stop
celluloid from self destructing
and collectors are on the look
out for information that will
help them preserve their collections. Because of celluloid's
fragile existence, many collectors turn to other more durable
materials. As collectors we
have been told to keep our celluloid combs exposed to air —
not enclosed behind glass.
Keep it cool, if possible, and
away from the sunlight. If dis-
played in a case use acid-free
materials to place the comb on
and hold it in place with stain-
less steel pins. Washing celluloid in warm soapy water
occasionally to clean away any
surface acidity is a good idea.
Waxing is discouraged as it
doesn't allow air to get to the
celluloid. A few drops of house-
hold ammonia in the water will
also help remove any acidity.

Exact dating of celluloid is
difficult because so few companies put their name or date on
their combs. Celluloid was popular between 1870 and 1920.
There were still celluloid
combs being made and worn

after that date, but in 1919 Irene Castle bobbed her hair and the comb industry was hurt to the point of no return. The majority of companies either closed or took up some other product to manufacture. Leominster, Massachusetts, was the center of comb making at that time, so it was probably hurt more than any other area in the country. The 50 years or so that celluloid combs were popular is a relatively short time to date their progress. With close study of the designs and different methods of decoration, we do have some idea where to place them in those years.

**Plate 1**

Pearlized, Art Deco, circa 1910 – 1930, 6½"w x 6½"h, $50.00 – 60.00.

**Plate 2**

Pearlized, late Art Nouveau, 1920s, 4"w x 2½"h, inscribed "Tortone," $30.00 – 35.00.

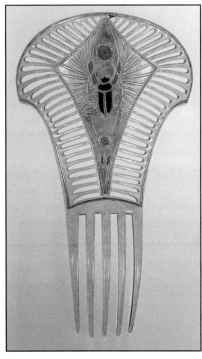

**Plate 4**
French ivory, circa 1920, 7"w x 8"h,
$60.00 – 75.00.

**Plate 3**
Pearlized, scarab design, Art
Deco, 1920s, 3¾"w x 6¾"h,
$60.00 – 75.00.

**Plate 5**
Circa 1901 – 1910,
pique d'or, 18K inlay,
3½"h x 4¼"w, $75.00
– 100.00.

**Plate 6**
Circa 1901 – 1910,
pique d'or, 18K inlay,
4"h x 5"w, $75.00 –
100.00.

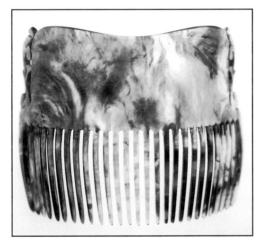

**Plate 7**
Faux tortoise, circa 1895,
3½"h x 4¼"w, $60.00 –
70.00.

**Plate 8**
Back comb, blonde,
pastes, claw settings,
4½"w    x    4½"h,
$65.00 – 75.00.

**Plate 9**
Black over clear with blue sets, circa 1890 – 1900, 5¼"w x 5¼"h, $50.00 – 60.00.

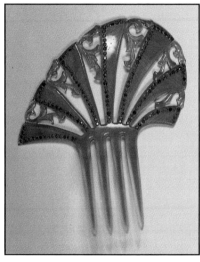

**Plate 10**
Pink pearlized, circa 1920, 4½"w x 5½"h, $45.00 – 55.00.

**Plate 11**
Back comb, clear and blue pastes, Art Nouveau, circa 1890 – 1910, 4"w x 4"h, $75.00 – 100.00.

**Plate 12**
Cut steel top fastened to a celluloid comb by thread, cut steel top late eighteenth century, 4½"w x 4"h, $50.00 – 60.00.

**Plate 13**
Close up of Plate 12.

**Plate 14**
Back comb, brass decorations with pastes, claw settings, Art Nouveau, circa 1890 – 1910, 4½"w x 3¼"h, $225.00 – 250.00.

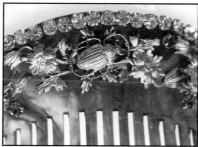

**Plate 15**
Close up of Plate 14.

**Plate 16**
Back comb, pique d'or, 22K gold inlay reg., circa 1901 – 1910, 3⅜"h x 4½"w, $85.00 – 95.00.

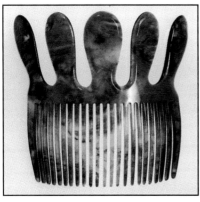

**Plate 18**
Back comb, circa 1880, 4¾"w x 3¼"h, $35.00 – 45.00.

**Plate 17**
Back comb, pastes, claw settings, circa 1890, 3½"h x 4"w, $75.00 – 100.00.

**Plate 19**
Back comb, circa 1890, brass lion, filigree, sets, 4¼"w x 3¼"h, $90.00 – 125.00.

**Plate 20**
Back comb, circa 1910, sets and pierced work, 5"w x 4"h, $50.00 – 60.00.

**Plate 21**
Back comb, circa 1918, eagle design in pastes, claw settings, 4½"w x 3½"h, $75.00 – 90.00.

**Plate 22**
Back comb, Art Nouveau, circa 1890 – 1910, 4½"w x 3"h, $90.00 – 100.00.

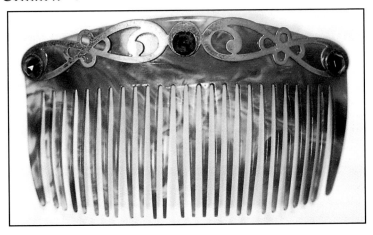

**Plate 23**
Back comb, Art Deco, circa
1920s, 4½"w x 2½"h, $35.00 –
40.00.

**Plate 24**
Back comb, circa 1930, 5"w
x 5"h, $40.00 – 50.00.

**Plate 25**
Back comb, Art Nouveau,
1890 – 1910, filigree,
pastes, 4½"w x 2¾"h,
$40.00 – 60.00.

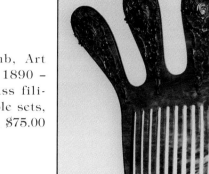

**Plate 26**
Back comb, Art Nouveau, 1890 – 1910, brass filigree, purple sets, 6"w x 5"h, $75.00 – 100.00.

**Plate 27**
Back comb, Art Deco, circa 1910 – 1930, etched gilt brass, gold color glass, 4½" x 2⅓"h, $50.00 – 70.00.

**Plate 28**
Back comb, pique d'or, 22K gold, trademark GW Reg., circa 1901 – 1910, $50.00 – 75.00.

**Plate 29**
Back comb, cast gilt brass fly, flowers, and leaves, pastes, Art Nouveau, 1890 – 1910, 4½"w x 3"h, $75.00 – 100.00.

**Plate 30**
Celluloid back comb, inscribed silver and gold deposit, 18K gold inlay, circa 1901 – 1910, $55.00 – 75.00.

**Plate 31**
Attached brass, chasing, amethyst or glass set, circa 1890 – 1910, $80.00 – 90.00.

**Plate 32**
Back comb, filigree and pastes, claw settings, circa 1900, 4"w x 3"h, $75.00 – 85.00.

**Plate 33**
Back comb, pierced work, gold paint, sets, Art Nouveau, circa 1890 – 1910, $50.00 – 65.00.

**Plate 34**
Pastes, claw settings, circa 1890, 2½"w x 2¾"h, $35.00 – 45.00.

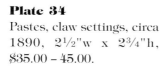

**Plate 35**
Back comb, filigree with pastes, claw settings, circa 1885, 4½"w x 3½"h, $50.00 –
60.00.

**Plate 36**
Small blue sets, Art Nouveau,
1890 – 1910, 3"w x 5"h, $40.00
– 50.00.

**Plate 37**
Bakelike fruit and scarabs, Art
Deco, 1910 – 1930, 4"w x 6"h,
$100.00 – 125.00.

20

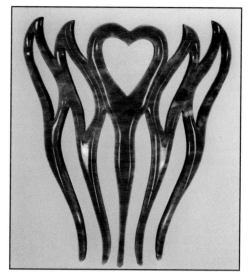

**Plate 38**
Heart design, Art Nouveau,
1910 – 1930, 4"w x 4¼"h,
$30.00 – 35.00.

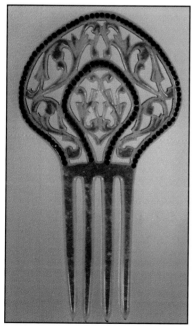

**Plate 40**
Faux tortoise, blue glass
sets, circa 1900, 3"w x 5"h,
$45.00 – 55.00.

**Plate 39**
Pierced work with blue glass
sets, circa 1900, 3¾"w x 5"h,
$50.00 – 60.00.

21

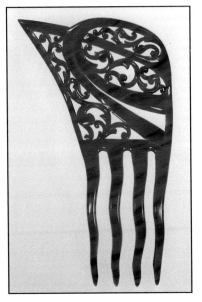

**Plate 41**
Faux tortoise, pierced work,
circa 1900, 3½"w x 6½"h,
$30.00 – 50.00.

**Plate 42**
Circa 1880, 3½"w x 5½"h,
$35.00 – 45.00.

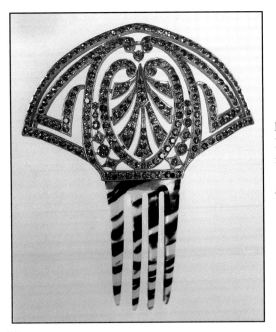

**Plate 43**
Faux tortoise with alu-
minum top, sets, circa
1890, 4½"w x 5½"h,
$80.00 – 90.00.

**Plate 44**
Faux tortoise with brass top, niello designed, 3½"h x 5½"w, $60.00 – 70.00.

**Plate 45**
Close up of Plate 44.

**Plate 46**
Faux tortoise pierced work, pavé arranged blue sets, Best-Hold inscribed, circa 1910, 6½"w x 7½"h, $65.00 – 75.00.

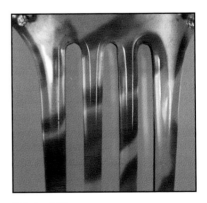

**Plate 48**
Back comb, faux tortoise, nicely arranged green and clear sets, circa 1910 – 1930, Art Deco, $45.00 – 55.00.

**Plate 47**
Faux tortoise, pavé set clear glass sets, circa 1910, 3½"w x 5½"h, $60.00 – 80.00.

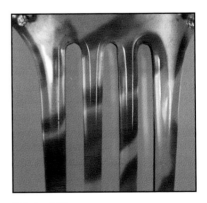

**Plate 50**
Close up of Plate 49 showing brushed-on dye.

**Plate 49**
Faux tortoise, circa 1890, clear sets, 2¾"w x 5"h, $35.00 – 45.00.

**Plate 51**
Faux tortoise, black and orange
sets, Art Deco, circa 1910 –
1930, 2½"w x 4½"h, if perfect
condition, $45.00 – 55.00.

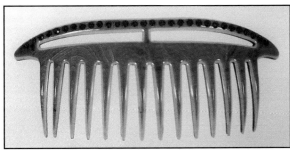

**Plate 52**
Comb or diadem,
blue watermarked
over clear, circa
1885, 5"w x 2½"h,
$70.00 – 80.00.

**Plate 53**
Comb or diadem, blue watermarked over clear, circa 1885,
8½"w x 3"h, $80.00 – 90.00.

**Plate 55**
Close up of Plate 54.

**Plate 54**
Blue watermarked over clear,
circa 1885, 5"w x 6¾"h, $165.00 –
175.00.

**Plate 57**
Close up of Plate 56.

**Plate 56**
Blue watermarked over clear,
pierced work, blue sets, circa
1885, 6"w x 7½"h, $165.00 –
175.00.

**Plate 58**
Red sets, Art Deco, 1910 – 1930, rounded to fit head, 3½"w x 5"h, $40.00 – 50.00.

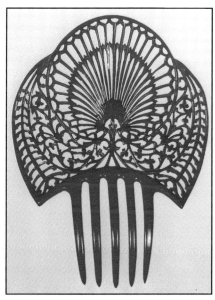

**Plate 59**
Pierced work, peacock motif, circa 1880 – 1890, 5"w x 6½"h, $65.00 – 75.00.

**Plate 60**
Red over clear, pierced work, red sets, circa 1880 – 1890, 5"w x 6¾"h, $120.00 – 130.00.

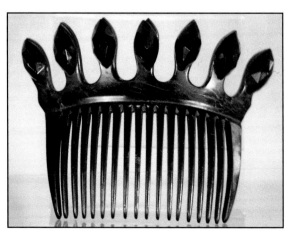

**Plate 62**
Black with French jet, circa 1890,
3½"w x 4¼"h, $50.00 – 60.00.

**Plate 61**
Coral color, pierced work, circa
1880 – 1890, 4"w x 7"h, $55.00 –
65.00.

**Plate 63**
Back comb, French jet, circa 1890, 4½"w x
3½"h, $40.00 – 55.00.

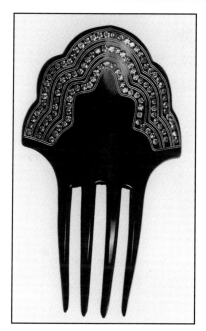

**Plate 64**
White paint in lines with clear sets on black, 3"w x 5"h, $35.00 – 40.00.

**Plate 65**
French jet, circa 1880 – 1890, 3¼"w x 6"h, $55.00 – 75.00.

**Plate 66**
French jet, circa 1880 – 1890, 4½"w x 3"h, $35.00 – 40.00.

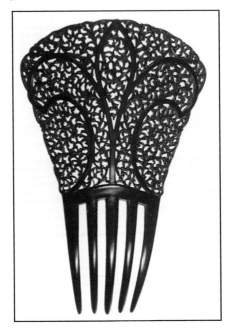

**Plate 67**
High back comb, fleur de lis pattern, circa 1880 – 1890, 4"w x 7"h, $55.00 – 75.00.

**Plate 69**
High back comb, pierced work, Art Deco, 1910 – 1930, 9"w x 8"h, $65.00 – 75.00.

**Plate 68**
Hinged with French jet, circa 1880 – 1890, 3"w x 3¼"h, $35.00 – 45.00.

**Plate 70**
Black sets, Art Deco, 1910 – 1930, 6"w x
7"h , $45.00 – 55.00.

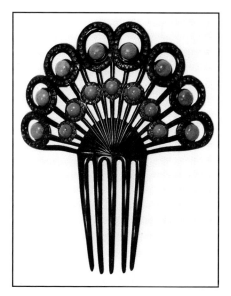

**Plate 71**
Art Deco, 1910 – 1930, 5"w x 6¼"h,
$65.00 – 75.00.

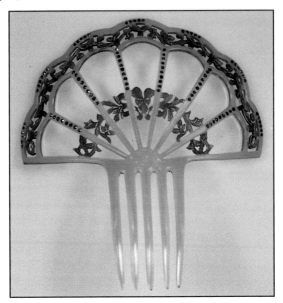

**Plate 72**
Fan motif, pierced work, circa 1880, 7½"w x
6¾"h, $50.00 – 60.00.

**Plate 73**
Black sets, circa 1880, 6"w x 6"h,
$50.00 – 60.00.

**Plate 74**
End of day mix of colors, circa 1880, 4"w x 5"h, $40.00 – 50.00.

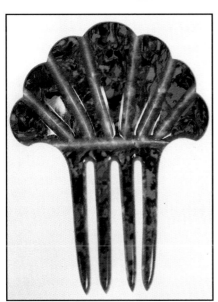

**Plate 75**
End of day mix of colors, circa 1880, 4"w x 5"h, $40.00 – 50.00.

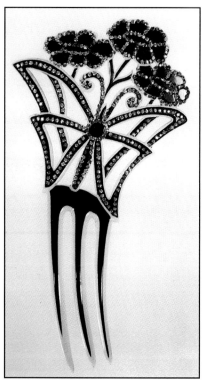

**Plate 77**
Black on clear, pierced work, circa 1880, 4½"w x 8½"h, $65.00 – 75.00.

**Plate 76**
Black on clear, butterfly motif, Art Nouveau, circa 1890 – 1910, 3½"w x 7"h, $90.00 – 100.00.

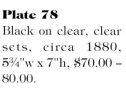

**Plate 78**
Black on clear, clear sets, circa 1880, 5¾"w x 7"h, $70.00 – 80.00.

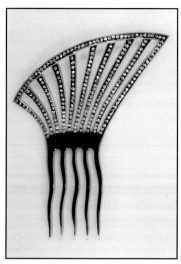

**Plate 80**
Fan motif, black on clear, circa 1880,
6½"w x 6"h, $50.00 – 60.00.

**Plate 79**
Black on clear, blue sets,
circa 1890 – 1910, 5"w x 7"h,
$100.00 – 110.00.

**Plate 81**
Black with red sets, circa 1895 –
1910, $50.00 – 60.00.

**Plate 82**
Black on clear, blue sets, circa 1890, 4½"w x 6"h, $40.00 – 50.00.

**Plate 83**
Black on clear, pink sets, circa 1890, 3½"w x 5"h, $40.00 – 45.00.

**Plate 84**
Black on clear, Art Deco, 3½"w x 5¼"h, $40.00 – 45.00.

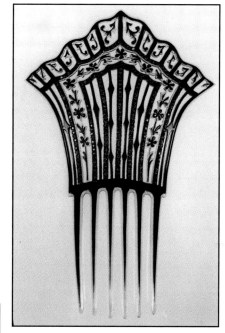

**Plate 85**
High back comb, black on clear, pierced work, green sets, circa 1880 – 1890, 5½"w x 8¼"h, $70.00 – 80.00.

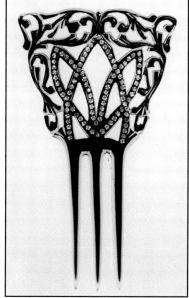

**Plate 86**
Black on clear, clear sets, circa 1880 – 1890, 3"w x 5"h, $45.00 – 55.00.

**Plate 87**
Black and cream with blue sets, circa 1920, 4½"w x 6½"h, $50.00 – 65.00.

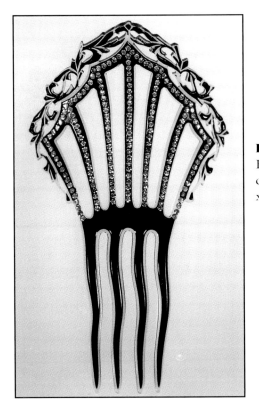

**Plate 88**
Black on clear, clear sets,
circa 1880 – 1890, 3½"w
x 6"h, $50.00 – 60.00.

**Plate 89**
Black on clear, fan
motif, circa 1880 –
1890, 8"w x 7"h,
$60.00 – 70.00.

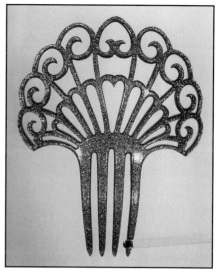

**Plate 90**
Black on clear, blue sets, Art Deco, circa, 1910 – 1930, 6½"w x 8"h, $160.00 – 175.00.

**Plate 91**
Imitation goldstone, Art Deco, circa 1910 – 1930, 4½"w x 5"h, $45.00 – 55.00.

**Plate 92**
Amber color with brass repoussé, Art Nouveau, circa 1890 – 1910, 5"w x 3"h, $40.00 – 50.00.

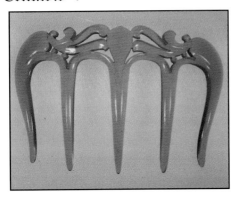

**Plate 93**
Amber color, circa 1895, 4"w x 3"h, $60.00 – 75.00.

**Plate 94**
Neck comb, amber color, circa 1895, 4½"w x 3"h , $45.00 – 55.00.

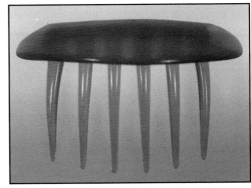

**Plate 95**
Filigree with French jet, Art Deco, 1910 – 1930, 3"w x 6"h, $50.00 – 65.00.

**Plate 96**
Back comb, amber color, circa 1900 – 1910, 5"w x 4"h, $40.00 – 45.00.

**Plate 97**
Amber color, filigree with fake coral flowers, pastes in claw settings, circa 1900 – 1910, 4"h x 4"w, $125.00 – 135.00.

**Plate 98**
Amber color with gold sets, circa 1880 – 1890, 3"w x 6¼"h, $45.00 – 55.00.

41

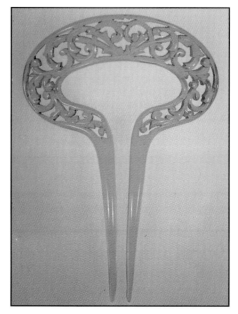

**Plate 99**
Amber, pierced work, circa 1880, 4"w
x 5"h, $30.00 – 35.00.

**Plate 100**
Back comb, amber with filigree and pastes with
claw settings, eagle motif, circa 1918, 5"w x
3"h, $100.00 – 120.00.

**Plate 101**
Fan shape with gold sets, TK in circle inscribed, Art Nouveau, circa 1890 – 1910, 7"w x 7"h, $75.00 – 80.00.

**Plate 102**
Clear, blue sets, Art Nouveau, circa 1890 – 1910, inscribed Best-Hold, 7"w x 7"h, $90.00 – 100.00.

43

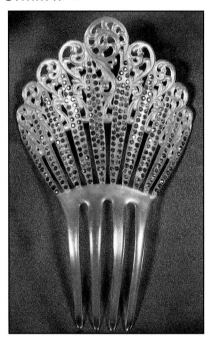

**Plate 103**
Clear with blue sets, circa
1880 – 1890, 4"w x 6½"h,
$45.00 – 55.00.

**Plate 104**
Clear with blue sets, circa 1880 – 1890,
6"w x 6½"h, $40.00 – 50.00.

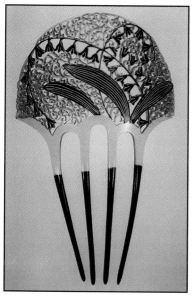

**Plate 105**
Clear with black lily of the valley motif, Art Nouveau, 1890 – 1910, 4"w x 7"h, $50.00 – 75.00.

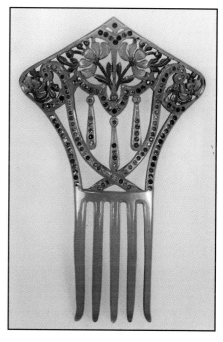

**Plate 106**
Cream with green sets, enamel flowers, Art Nouveau, 1890 – 1910, 4"w x 5½"h, $50.00 – 60.00.

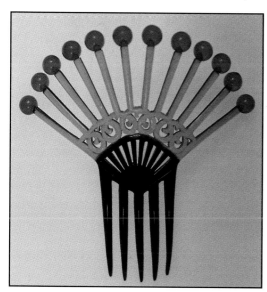

**Plate 107**
Amber and black, Art Deco, 1910 – 1930, 6"w x 6"h, $150.00 – 160.00.

## Plate 108
Amber and black, parrot motif, circa 1880 – 1890, 8"w x 7½"h, $90.00 – 125.00.

## Plate 109
Red and black, Art Deco, circa 1910 – 1930, 4½"w x 5¾"h, $70.00 – 80.00.

## Plate 110
Black and white with clear sets, parrot motif, circa 1880 – 1890, 6½"w x 6¾"h, $100.00 – 120.00

**Plate 111**
Comb or diadem, French ivory, red sets, Art Nouveau, circa 1890 – 1910, 5½"w x 3"h, $55.00 – 65.00.

**Plate 112**
Back comb, pearlized top layer, pierced work with clear sets, circa 1920, 5¼"w x 4"h, $60.00 – 75.00.

**Plate 113**
French ivory with black, inscribed Kroko, Art Deco, circa 1910 – 1930, 2½"w x 6"h, $80.00 – 90.00.

47

**Plate 114**
French ivory, circa
1920, 5½"w x 6"h,
$50.00 – 60.00.

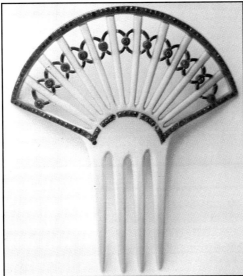

**Plate 115**
Clear and blue sets,
French ivory, circa
1920, 5½"w x 7½"h,
$65.00 – 75.00.

**Plate 116**
Close up of Plate 115
showing French ivory
pattern.

**Plate 117**
High back comb, pierced work,
French ivory, circa 1880 – 1890,
5"w x 8½"h, $60.00 – 85.00.

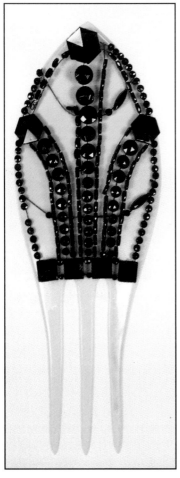

**Plate 118**
High comb, French ivory,
French jet on wire, circa 1880
– 1890, 3"w x 8"h, as is
$45.00.

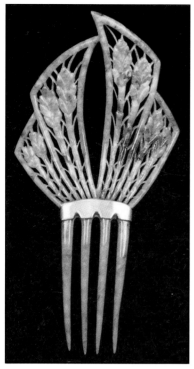

**Plate 119**
Oats motif, sterling band, Art
Nouveau, 1890 – 1910, 3½"w x
6½"h, $65.00 – 75.00.

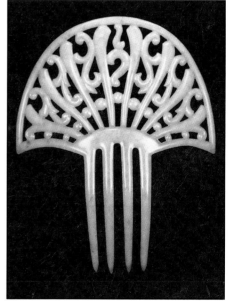

**Plate 120**
Celedon green, circa 1880 – 1890,
4¾"w x 4¾"h, $45.00 – 55.00.

**Plate 121**
Pique d'or, 18K gold
inlayed, $80.00 – 90.00.

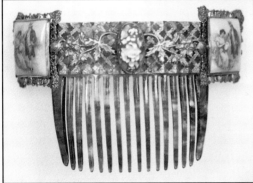

**Plate 122**
Back comb with brass
and decals on porcelain
inserted, 3"h x 5"w,
$140.00 – 150.00.

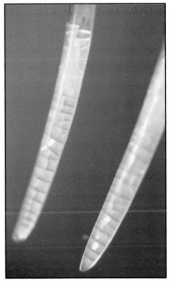

**Plate 123**
Enlargement of cellu-
loid in a phase of dete-
rioration.

# Tortoise Shell

One of the first things comb collectors learn about tortoise shell is that it doesn't come from a tortoise, but from a turtle. According to Webster's Dictionary the word turtle applies to sea turtles and tortoise is used for land turtles. The hawksbill turtle is from the sea. Why the shell is called tortoise shell is unknown. The hawksbill turtle is from tropical waters, especially near the islands of the Pacific. Its horn shell is from $\frac{1}{8}$ to $\frac{1}{4}$ of an inch thick. The plates are usually mottled, with no two alike. The bottom of the turtle's shell is a blonde color and usually without markings. Since there was so little of the shell obtained from the bottom, there were less items made from it. A blonde tortoise shell comb is quite rare, and consequently very expensive.

In *Comb Making in America*, Bernard Doyle wrote, "The turtle's plates are removed by heat from the back of the living turtle after which he is thrown back into the sea in order that other plates may grow." If the blond or bottom part of the shell was used, the turtle died. After removal, the shell was softened in boiling water and then common table salt was added to set the color and prevent fading. The plates were flattened by heat and pressure and all irregularities were scraped away using a rasp. To make pieces large enough for some projects, two pieces of shell could be overlapped and with low heat and pressure the two pieces would bond. The shell surface liquifies causing the pieces to become one. Laying two pieces, one upon the other, using the same method of low heat and pressure, a thicker piece could be obtained. Some combs make you wonder how they were achieved. Tortoise shell was more brittle than horn, but it was easy to carve. It could be twisted and shaped as well. After cutting out a comb by using a pattern, an engraver would do the final carving and detail work. Moistened brick dust was used to smooth the shell and then polished with rotten stone, chalk, and vinegar.

Tortoise shell was used in the early 1700s until around

1860, when it was no longer popular. Horn was used in its place as it was cheaper and could be made to look like tortoise shell. The hawkesbill turtle is protected now as its survival as a species was becoming threatened.

When purchasing tortoise shell you will frequently find small chips on the surface, especially along the edges of the teeth, but it won't deteriorate like celluloid. Tortoise that has become dull from use or age can be brightened by using mineral oil or Vaseline. To keep it bright use a good polish such as Cimichrome.

**Plate 124**
Three rows of chain, circa 1810, 5½"w x 4½"h, $400.00 – 500.00.

**Plate 125**
High back comb, pierced work, circa 1850, 4"w x 6½"h, $45.00 – 55.00.

53

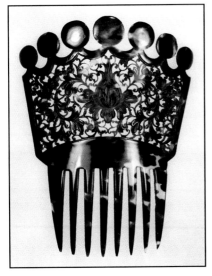

**Plate 126**
Back comb, pierced work, circa
1830, 5½"w x 2¼"h, $300.00 –
400.00.

**Plate 127**
Oriental pierced work, circa 1850,
5½"w x 9½"h, $100.00 – 125.00.

**Plate 128**
Leaf shape, circa 1887, 3¼"w x
6"h, $50.00 – 60.00.

**Plate 129**
Folding comb, three leaves, hinged, circa 1850, 5"w, x 3"h, $65.00 – 75.00.

**Plate 130**
View of Plate 129 folded.

**Plate 131**
Plain, circa 1887, 5¼"w x 6½"h, $55.00 – 65.00.

**Plate 132**
Cut work, three stars, circa 1850, 4¼"w x 5"h, $50.00 – 55.00.

**Plate 133**
Plain, circa 1887, 3½"w x 5¾"h, $60.00 – 70.00.

**Plate 134**
High back comb, circa 1830, 4½"w x 7"h, $350.00 – 400.00.

**Plate 136**
Cut work, circa 1887, 5"w x 6¾"h,
$65.00 – 75.00.

**Plate 135**
Oriental, carved dragon pattern, circa 1810, 3"w x 8"h,
$250.00 – 275.00.

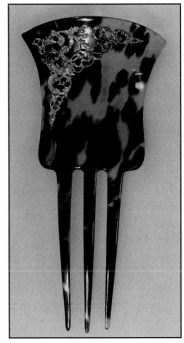

**Plate 137**
Hair decoration, gold
pattern attached, circa
1895, 3¼"w x 5½"h,
$100.00 – 125.00.

**Plate 138**
Blonde comb, original box, circa 1860, 4¼"w x 4½"h, $400.00 – 450.00.

**Plate 139**
Plain, circa 1887, 4"w x 5"h, $50.00 – 60.00.

**Plate 140**
Plain, circa 1887, 4½"w x 5¾"h, $50.00 – 60.00.

**Plate 141**
Plain (dull finish), circa 1887,
2¾"w x 5"h, $35.00 – 45.00.

**Plate 142**
Cut work, circa 1850, 4"w x
8"h, $50.00 – 60.00.

**Plate 143**
Blonde, nine balls on top,
circa 1850, 3½"w x 4"h,
$150.00 – 200.00.

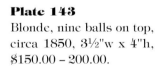

**Plate 144**
Parure (matching set) in original box, Japanese,
$350.00 – 400.00.

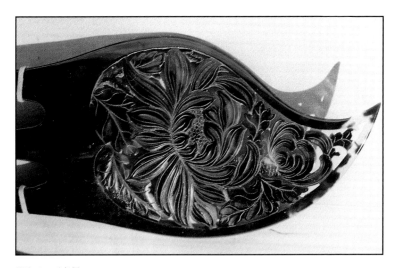

**Plate 145**
Close up of design of Plate 144.

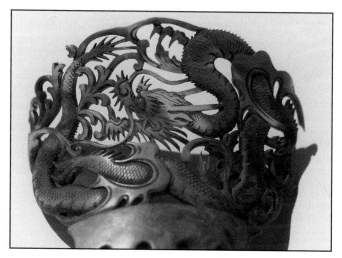

**Plate 146**
Top of old comb, teeth damaged, Oriental carving,
$35.00.

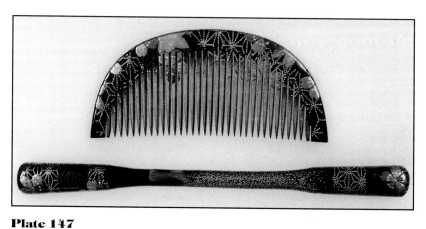

**Plate 147**
Japanese Kusi (comb) and Kogai (bar), cobwebs and cherry blossom
design, original box included, $250.00 – 300.00.

# Metal

**S**ilver. Silver is probably the most common precious metal used for jewelry, and its use is centuries old. Silver is a white metal and can be easily worked because it is relatively soft. Chasing, engraving, and piercing were already being used as early as 4000 BC. Most silver is a by-product of the refining of other metals. There are small amounts found all over the world. There are, however, places where it is more abundant, such as Taxco, Mexico, which has a large silver jewelry industry. Although a very durable metal, exposure to sulfur in the air will turn silver black. Copper is added to silver to harden it. The government controls the amount used. In the fourteenth century Edward I set the standard for sterling silver in England. It had to have a hallmark or be stamped with punches to give its silver content. Sterling silver must have 92½ percent silver and 7½ percent copper. Sterling silver is used for all kinds of jewelry, good flatware, bowls, and vases. Coin silver is a mixture of 90 percent silver and 10 percent copper. Mexican silver is usually above 90 percent silver.

Jewelry with silver plate is not very practical as the silver wears away leaving the base metal bare.

There are methods to test the silver content. I would take most jewelry to a jeweler who will have the proper materials for testing. If a piece does have an inconspicuous place to scratch into the metal, a drop of nitric acid on the cut will cause the silver to turn different colors by which you can figure the silver content. Sterling silver will turn a cream color, while coin silver will turn dark or black. A scratch in silver plate will reveal the base metal, usually brass, which will turn green.

Silver can be brightened with a good silver polish. I avoid polishing my sterling pieces too often by wrapping them in clear plastic wrap as you can still see the comb while protecting it.

**B**rass. Brass is an alloy of copper and zinc. Changing the amounts of both metals will change the color of the resulting brass. Gilded brass, as used in most combs, was 95 percent copper and five percent zinc. By using 15 percent zinc to 85 percent copper, the brass will take on a reddish cast. Brass can be cast, welded, stamped, and filed. It often was used in the embellishment of combs. Brass was also used as a base metal for gold-plated items. A method called niello was used to decorate brass as described in the Celluloid chapter.

**S**teel and Cut Steel Studs. I have a steel comb made with a cut-out design with no added materials to decorate it. These are not particularly attractive, but probably were inexpensive and served the purpose of decorating the hair for the lady who could not afford a more elaborate comb.

Cut steel studs were just that. They were riveted to the base metal that was then added to the comb. They were faceted and usually placed fairly close to each other giving a nice sparkle to the comb. The comb could be any material with the studs added. The steel sets were generally crudely done. When examined closely, one can see they are not all alike. The steel studs do tend to rust so samples are not always in the best condition. This form of decoration was made in the early 1800s and continued to be used until around 1850. I purchased one comb with a beautiful top of cut steel. When I arrived home

I realized the top was attached to a celluloid comb base by threads. Steel studs were not used on celluloid, but were most apt to be found on horn or steel combs. How easy to be carried away! The top was so attractive I didn't examine the rest of the comb.

**A**luminum. Aluminum is a bluish silver white malleable metal, very light in weight and resistant to oxidation. It is the most abundant metallic element and always occurs in combination with other metals. Combs made of aluminum were fairly simple in design but the tops could have marcasite or glass sets imbedded. Occasionally horn, tortoise, and even celluloid will have an added aluminum top. They were first made in early nineteenth century and are not very plentiful today, even though they continued to be used until around 1900.

**G**old. Webster's Dictionary describes gold as "a soft, yellow, corrosion-resistant element, the most malleable and ductile metal, occurring in veins and alluvial deposits, and recovered by mining or by panning or sluicing." Gold is a precious metal used since antiquity. It is very durable and was used in both hairpins and combs. Sterling silver was sometimes plated with gold – jewelers will refer to this as vermeil. An all gold piece will be quite expensive due to the price of gold today. It is more apt to be found in the trim of a hair ornament, as inlay or fili-gree. In the seventh century it was used in a granulated form incorporated into a design. Occasional hairpins can be found that are 14K gold, but most combs of this value will be found in museums, and not available to collectors.

**Plate 148**
Sterling comb, filigree and star design, circa 1850, 1½"w x 4"h, $40.00 – 50.00.

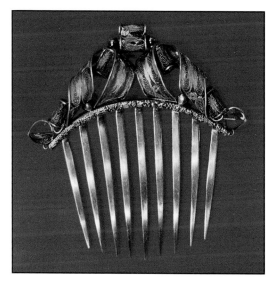

**Plate 149**
Sterling, filigree, 4"w x 4"h, $115.00 –
125.00.

**Plate 150**
Enlargement of Plate 149.

**Plate 151**
Sterling, Oriental back comb, 4"w x 4"h, $55.00 – 65.00.

**Plate 152**
Silverplate, repoussé design, 5"w x 5"h,
$35.00 – 45.00.

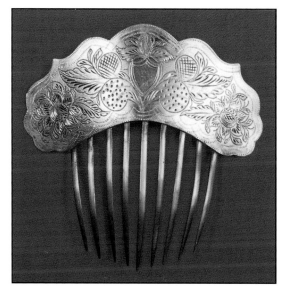

**Plate 153**
Coin silver, engraved design, circa 1850, 5"w x
4½"h, $30.00 – 40.00.

**Plate 154**
Sterling, engraved design, 4¼"w x 4½"h,
$120.00 – 130.00.

**Plate 155**
Cut steel, embossed, circa 1810,
4"w x 5"h, $45.00 – 55.00.

**Plate 156**
Brass, 3"w x 3¼"h,
$25.00 – 35.00.

## Plate 157

Silver gilt, filigree, circa 1800 – 1810, 4¾"w x 5"h, $75.00 – 85.00.

## Plate 158

Coin silver, etched with eight movable balls, circa 1800 – 1810, 3¾"w x 6"h, $65.00 – 75.00.

**Plate 159**
Sterling, cut work and etched, 4¼"w x 6½"h, $200.00 – 225.00.

**Plate 160**
Sterling, contemporary, hollow lion, 2"w x 4"h, $40.00 – 50.00.

**Plate 161**
Steel, chased, cut work, wire teeth, 4"w x 4½"h, circa 1810, $35.00 – 45.00.

70

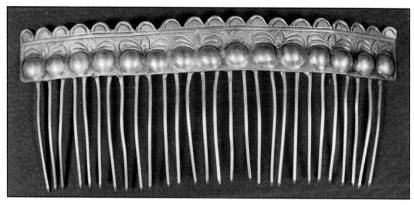

**Plate 162**
Sterling, oriental, 5"w x 2"h, $45.00 – 55.00.

**Plate 163**
Aluminum, origin unknown, handmade, 4¼"w x 1½"h, $10.00 – 15.00.

**Plate 164**
Sterling, celluloid teeth, cut
work, circa 1900 – 1910, 2½"w x
4½"h, $65.00 - 75.00.

**Plate 165**
Sterling, initial "C," gold wash,
2½"w x 4"h, $40.00 – 50.00.

**Plate 166**
Sterling, cut work, Art Nouveau, circa 1904 – 1906, 2¼"w x 5½"h, $90.00 – 100.00.

**Plate 167**
Brass hair ornament, 2½"w x 4½"h, $45.00 – 55.00.

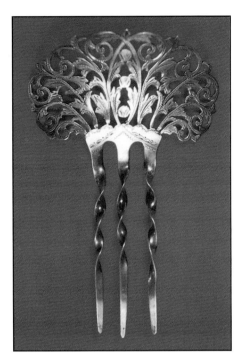

**Plate 168**
Sterling hair orna-
ment, cut work, circa
1904 – 1906, 3½"w x
5¼"h,  $75.00  –
85.00.

**Plate 169**
Sterling, from Dodge Estate,
Michigan, designed front and
back, 3¼"w x 5"h, $160.00 –
175.00.

**Plate 170**
Steel, chasing, circa
1810, 3½"w x 5"h,
$40.00 – 45.00.

**Plate 171**
Steel, chasing, circa 1810, 4½"w x 5¼"h,
$35.00 – 45.00.

**Plate 172**
Brass, filigree, and
cut steel studs, circa
1860, 3¼"w x 5"h,
$35.00 – 45.00.

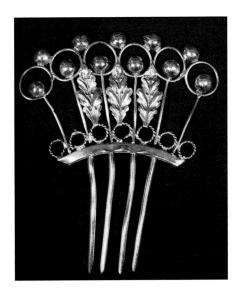

**Plate 173**
Sterling, with three oak leaves, 4¼"w
x 5"h, $50.00 – 60.00.

**Plate 174**
Cast-iron, interesting, information welcome, 2¼"h x 4½"w, $50.00 – 60.00.

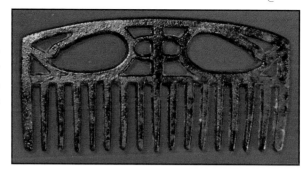

**Plate 175**
Coin silver, Oriental, 2"h x 4½"w, $35.00 – 45.00.

**Plate 176**
Gilt brass with niello work, circa 1840, 2½"w x 5½"h, $45.00 – 55.00.

**Plate 177**
Sterling, embossed, circa 1850, 3"w x
3½"h, $60.00 – 70.00.

**Plate 178**
Silver plate, from the
Sumba Island Royal Col-
lection, ¾"w x 6¼"h,
$280.00 – 300.00.

# Horn

The use of horn in making various items is centuries old. In the thirteenth century craftsmen formed guilds, which were similar in aim to our unions today. Like trades would group together to establish some protection for its tradesmen, trying to keep their business confined to their own guild. The horn craftsmen were divided into two groups, but the guild had authority over both. The lowliest job was the horn presser who had to be of tough stature to be able to press the horn into flat pieces. The horn was cut into several rings and held over a fire until it was soft and then it was pried open. It was placed between hot iron plates that were pressed until the desired thickness was achieved. It was then cooled. The flattened pieces were described as leaves and plates. The finished product needed to be scraped, trimmed, and polished before it was sent on to the "horner." His position was a step above the horn presser and required more expertise in making the many items used in those days. The plates and leaves were either pressed into molds as for buttons, or made into drinking cups, powder horns, ink horns, hunter's horns, and combs. Horn that was pressed so thin it became translucent was used in place of glass, which was very scarce and expensive. Horn was used for lanterns as well as windows. In the 1580s glass became easier to get so the use of horn declined, but it was still used heavily for lanterns.

References seem to differ some as to whether hot water or hot oil was used to soften the horn, or as stated above it was held in the fire. I rather expect all were used at some time over the years. The heating and softening of the horn was done frequently in people's homes in the fireplace which was their source of heat and where all their cooking was done. The smell was very offensive as this process could take up to five hours, and was sometimes going on continually. Steer horn was the most useful because of its size. Other horns which were used are cow horn, buffalo, and even hooves were used in Scotland and England. Most of these were not nearly as satisfactory as the steer horn as some were brittle or the wrong size. In West Newbury and Worcestershire there were several tanneries where the supply of horns was usually sufficient. In the earlier years horns could be collected from nearby farmers.

In the United States in 1759, Enoch Noyes, as a young man, started the comb industry in West Newbury, Massachusetts. Although he started making horn combs, he also used tortoise shell, as the process for preparation was quite similar. In those early days the process of making one comb was a long laborious job. Each tooth was sawed by hand, and then smoothed on the edges. Enoch Noyes also created the case comb. At first this was a very crudely formed thing, but it developed later into some quite lovely case combs, some made of silver or mother of pearl with a celluloid or tortoise-shell comb.

Around 1805 there was a demand for a better product so the horners used a process called clarifying which made the horn translucent and turned it a nice amber color. They also used dyes to color the horn, usually a darker brown. During these years they would dye the horn to resemble tortoise shell, which

was harder to get. Various other means were used to decorate the combs. Materials that have been used to attach to the tops are sterling silver, lead, aluminum, brass, and French jet. A few combs will be found that are more than one piece of horn attached to each other by small wire pins. The metal tops were decorated by chasing, piercing, and repoussé. The patterns in the horn itself were usually quite geometric and simple. The hinged comb was an innovation developed during the middle to latter part of the nineteenth century. When celluloid, in 1870, became the material of choice, the use of horn declined rapidly.

Horn can be recognized by looking at the grain. As horn has an outer layer made up of keratin, the surface will show fine parallel lines. If that isn't sufficient to recognize horn, run hot water over it or take small shavings from a tooth and give it the flame test. This will give off an odor similar to burnt hair. By looking at the edges of a comb tooth you may see signs of layering or even signs of peeling. These are sure signs of horn. A little mineral oil on horn will help preserve it as it can become brittle with age.

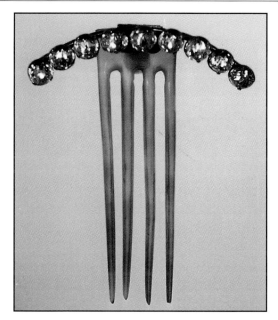

**Plate 179**
Hinged, large pastes, 2½"w x 4"h, $35.00 –
45.00.

**Plate 180**
Carved, cut out, Mexican, 5"w x 2¾"h, $30.00 – 40.00.

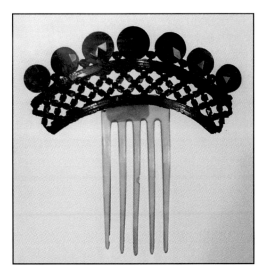

**Plate 181**

French jet, damaged, 4"w x 4"h, $15.00 – 20.00.

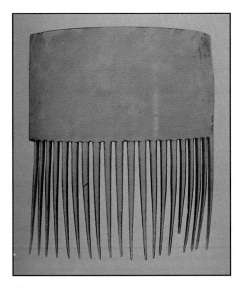

**Plate 182**

Clarified, lightly dyed, 4¾"w x 5½"h, $45.00 – 55.00.

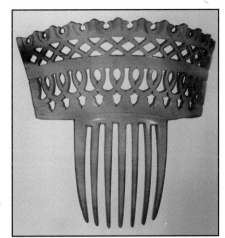

**Plate 183**
Clarified, early 1800s,
4½"w x 4"h, $30.00 –
40.00.

**Plate 184**
Brass grapes, leaves, 3¼"w x 2"h, $10.00 – 20.00.

# Horn

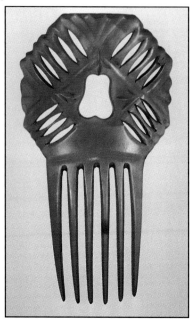

**Plate 185**
Dyed, 3"w x 5½"h, $45.00 –
55.00.

**Plate 186**
Clarified, dyed, circa 1860, 4"w x
5½"h, $25.00 – 30.00.

**Plate 187**
Hand designed, early 1800s, $100.00 – 125.00.

84

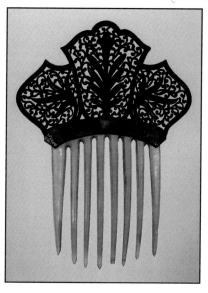

**Plate 188**
Dyed to resemble tortoise, 3½"w
x 5"h, $55.00 – 65.00.

**Plate 189**
Clarified with lead-pierced top,
early 1800s, 3½"w x 4¼"h,
$110.00 – 120.00.

**Plate 190**
Natural color, 2¼"w x
4"h, $20.00 – 25.00.

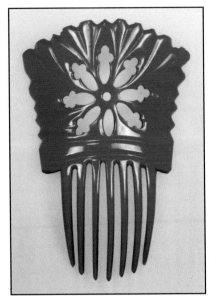

**Plate 191**
Dyed magenta, 3½"w x 4½"h,
$50.00 – 60.00.

**Plate 192**
Dyed black, bangles and hinged, 4"w x 4"h,
$90.00 – 100.00.

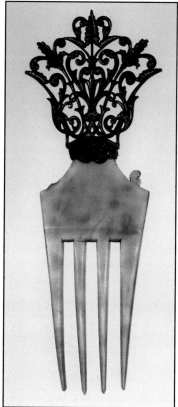

**Plate 193**
Sterling cutwork top, 2"w x 5½"h, $40.00 – 45.00.

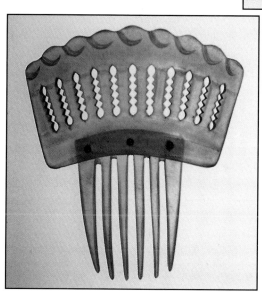

**Plate 194**
Cut work, clarified, two pieces pinned together, early 1800s, 3½"w x 4½"h, $35.00 – 45.00.

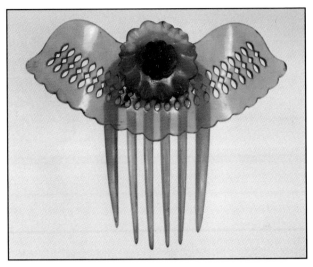

**Plate 195**
Cut work, clarified, hinged, early 1800s, 4"w x 3½"h, $40.00 – 50.00.

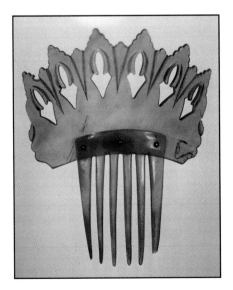

**Plate 196**
Clarified, cut work, early 1800s, 4"w x 4½"h, $55.00 – 65.00.

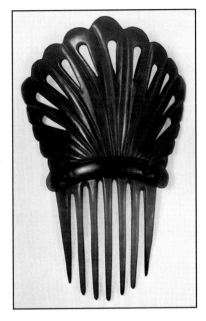

**Plate 197**
Dyed, cut work, late
1700s, 3½"w x 5½"h,
$50.00 – 60.00.

**Plate 198**
Clarified, cut work,
early 1800s, 4½"w x
4½"h, $35.00 – 45.00.

**Plate 199**
Dyed, cut work, probably faceted
ebonite balls, 3½"w x 5½"h,
$60.00 – 70.00.

**Plate 200**
Dyed, cut work, late 1700s, 4½"w
x 6¼"h, $75.00 – 85.00.

**Plate 201**
Cut work, mid-1800s, 4¼"w
x 6½"h, $75.00 – 85.00.

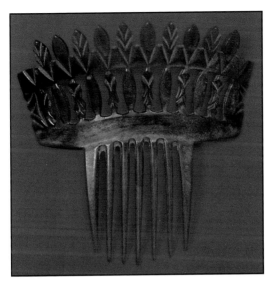

**Plate 202**
Dyed, cutwork, 4"w x 4"h, $65.00 – 75.00.

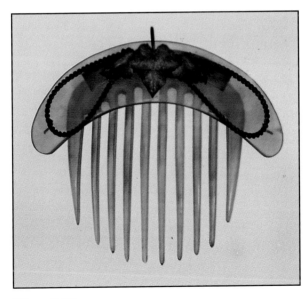

**Plate 203**
Hinged, 3½"w x 3"h, $45.00 – 55.00.

**Plate 204**
Hinged, 2½"w x 3"h, $45.00 – 55.00.

# Ivory

We are all familiar with ivory and its beautiful carvings. Being a natural material it was readily available and used as early as the Stone Age. Water can't penetrate ivory so many pieces have survived the centuries.

Before power tools came into being, around 1900, the simple ax and adz were used to remove the outer layer of the tusk which was then cut into sections. Hand chisels, fretsaws, and gauges were employed for the carving. After 1900 dental tools were used.

Although elephant tusks were the main source for ivory, the Encyclopedia Brittanica lists other sources: "the teeth of hippo, walrus, narwhal, sperm whale, and some types of boars." Most of these animals don't produce enough horn to make it worth-while to use commercially. The male elephant from India is the only one with tusks large enough to be of use. By using a loupe you can see the pattern of the ivory. A definite pattern can be seen in African ivory while ivory from India is much tighter grained and more difficult to see.

Prior to the second century A.D., elephants were plentiful in Asia. As a result of the increased population and hunting, the herds moved on to Southwest China. The Arab traders soon filled the demand gap by sending African ivory from Zanzibar to China. At this time elephants are protected.

Bernard W. Doyle, in his book *Comb Making in America* states that, "ivory combs were first made in this country about 1789 by Andrew Lord of Saybrook, Connecticut, who cut the plates and the teeth with a hand saw."

Of all of the ivory combs I have seen, the most beautiful are the Oriental ones. I do have one unusual ivory comb that I treasure. It has a sterling silver band with tiger claws at the top. It could be one of a kind. India is probably the place of origin because of the closeness of the grain in the ivory and the fact that tigers are prevalent in that country.

**Plate 205**
Ivory and sterling comb with tiger claws, 3"w x 5"h, $400.00 – 500.00.

**Plate 206**
Carved, 2"w x 4½"h, $35.00 – 40.00.

**Plate 207**
Carved, probably African,
3"w x 4¾"h, $40.00 – 50.00.

**Plate 208**
Close up of Plate 207, showing
grain of African ivory.

**Plate 209**
Two similar ivory combs, carved, 1¼"w x 2"h and 1½"w x 2¼"h, $15.00 each.

**Plate 210**
"H" comb, prior to the tenth century, probably central Europe, 2½"h x 3"w, $1,000.00.

# Wood, Vulcanite & Utility

ood. Both Oriental and African combs can be found made of different woods local to the region they are made. Combs from both of these areas are not easily found in this country. It seems Ghana has more combs available than other parts of Africa. To date them is very difficult, as they could still be making them for trade.

ulcanite. Vulcanite or vulcanized rubber was patented in 1844 by Charles Goodyear. Rubber is a natural resin and when heated and put under pressure, sulfur is added. The soft mass will become less sticky, stronger, and more resilient so it can be molded. Vulcanite became a popular substance to make utilitarian combs, but was used to make simple decorative combs as well. Not a lot of them are to be found, and with the natural aging process they become quite dull and take on a slightly yellowish cast. When testing rub with your fingers and you should smell a slight hint of sulfur. It is best not to expose vulcanite to heat as it will only hasten the aging of the comb.

**Plate 211**
Wooden comb from Ghana, Africa, $125.00.

97

**Plate 212**
Wooden comb from Ghana,
Africa, $133.00.

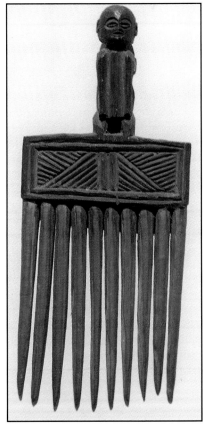

**Plate 213**
Wooden comb from Africa, $65.00.

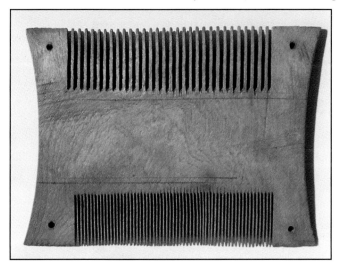

**Plate 214**
Wooden "H" comb, $15.00.

**Plate 215**
Pair of combs, Africa, 3½"w x ¼"h, $35.00.

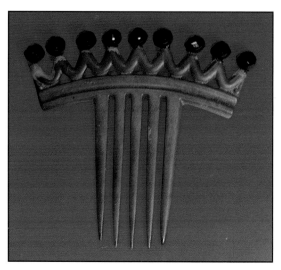

**Plate 216**
Vulcanite comb with jet faceted balls, circa 1900, $25.00.

**Plate 217**
Vulcanite comb, molded, circa 1900, $20.00.

**Plate 218**
Vulcanite comb, circa 1900, $35.00 – 45.00.

**Plate 219**
Vulcanite comb, circa 1900, $15.00.

**Plate 220**
Vulcanite comb, inscribed Goodyear,
circa 1900, $15.00.

**Plate 221**
Vulcanite comb, French jet faceted balls, circa 1900,
$25.00.

**Plate 222**
Vulcanized rubber, 3"w x 6"h,
$50.00 – 75.00.

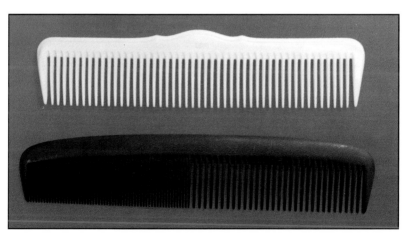

**Plate 223**
Top: French ivory utility comb, circa 1920, $15.00.
Bottom: Hard rubber, vulcanite utility comb, circa 1900, $5.00.

**Plate 224**
Unusual utility comb, inscribed Made in France, depose, $50.00.

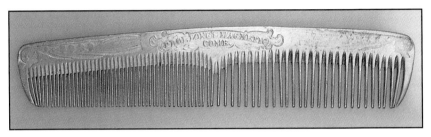

**Plate 225**
Aluminum utility comb, inscribed Prof. Longe Magnetic Comb, $8.00.

**Plate 226**
Woven comb from the Pacific islands, $35.00.

# Hairpins

airpins as we know them, with two prongs, were in use by about 1770. Previous to this time a hairpin had only one prong called a bodkin. Women of the eighteenth century used a cushion on top of their heads to support the tall coiffures that were popular at that time. They were most popular in France although the English were soon copying them. The structures needed all sorts of help to keep them in place. Hairpins along with pomatum and white powder helped hold the lady's hair up over the supporting cushion. Pomatum was a sticky substance similar to our hair spray used today. Women weren't content just to have elaborate hairdos but added to the top miniature gardens with both real or artificial flowers, a ship in full sail, or a windmill with farm animals. Added to the arrangements were strings of pearls and feathers. Writers of the day spent a lot of time ridiculing these hairdos, both in poetry and prose. The women often left their hair in these arrangements for months without cleaning, so that lice became a problem. Antique dealers of today sell an item they call a back scratcher. In reality the ladies used it to scratch their heads. The height of the hair also caused a problem when they rode in a carriage. They would lean out of the side of the carriage to avoid ruining the hair arrangement.

The original hairpins were simple in design and were strictly functional. Later designers followed the trends of combs of the day by adding many kinds of treatments to glorify the hairpin and to make it decorative as well as useful. The comb with three teeth is a "hair ornament" to differentiate it from the hairpin, with two teeth, and the comb has four or more teeth. The hairpins in my collection represent all of the materials I have described previously and show many of the different ways the hairpin was decorated.

Some of the Oriental hairpins have two long metal prongs with added brass flowers, bangles, and tremblants to beautify them. The Japanese call them Kanzasi. Tremblants were tiny springs that might represent the feelers on a butterfly. Sometimes they had objects added at the end of the spring, such as jade beads, that would bounce as the wearer walked. The Kanzasi were prevalent during the Edo period, 1603 to 1867. The Kanzasi found today will be from the latter part of the Edo period as they were quite fragile. Many of these hairpins had "ear spoons" extending beyond the top. They cleaned the wax out of their ears with the ear spoon or even used them to scratch their head. There was a period in which the government wouldn't allow anything that was decorative to be worn, so the ear spoons were added to make it a utilitarian piece.

In China they made hairpins using kingfisher bird's feathers. The kingfisher bird was quite small but with brilliant blue feathers. The designers cut the feathers into tiny pieces and fastened them to the metal in lovely patterns. The kingfisher bird became almost extinct from over use. Many of the hairpins found today will have some of the feathers missing. To discover one complete is a real find. Evelyn Haertig mentions in her book, *Combs & Purses*, that combs with kingfisher feathers can still be found in China at reasonable prices. They are less attainable here in the U. S.

Garnets and amber are among the popular decorations on hairpins. Most hairpins with garnets have hinges. They were popular from 1830 on. In jewelry stores in New Orleans I saw a lot of garnet hairpins, all priced well above $300. Amber found on combs was usually in the form of faceted balls. Horn and tortoise shell made up the main part of the comb or pin. So-called amber combs are probably amber colored celluloid or clarified horn and not amber at all.

Brilliants of one kind or another decorate many of the hairpins in my collection. These were popular in the early part of the twentieth century to as late as the 1940s and added a bit of glitter to a lady's evening costume.

Hairpins make up a large part of my collection. I find them to be even more varied in materials than my combs. Most hairpins are quite reasonable in price. Occasionally there will be one in perfect condition and unusual enough to warrant a considerable price.

∾

Hairpins are usually between 3 – 5" in height, with the exception of the Japanese Kanzasi, which can be as much as 8".

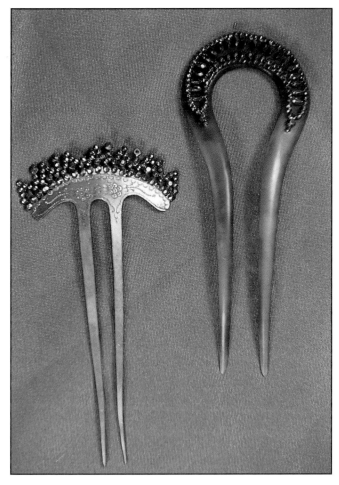

**Plate 227**

Left: steel, cut steel studs, circa 1760 – 1800, $60.00 – 70.00; right: horn, faux tortoise, cut steel decoration, circa 1760 – 1800, $50.00 – 60.00.

**Plate 228**
From left: pair of brass hairpins, blue beads, circa 1910, $20.00
– 25.00; brass, $20.00 – 25.00; brass, blue set, $25.00 – 30.00.

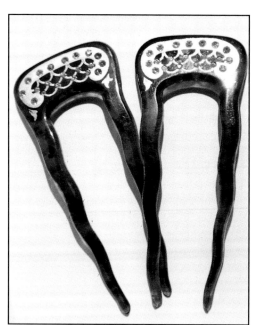

**Plate 229**
Pair of celluloid hairpins, 18K gold inlaid, Art Deco, 1910 – 1930, $45.00 – 55.00.

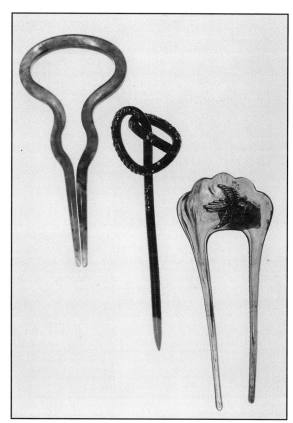

**Plate 230**
Celluloid, circa 1920, $5.00 – 7.50; celluloid, abalone insets, $2.00 – 3.00; celluloid, attached brass pheasant, $5.00 – 7.50.

**Plate 231**
Celluloid, Chinese two-piece, circa 1910, $30.00 – 40.00.

**Plate 232**
Sterling, inscribed
Tosco, $55.00 – 60.00.

**Plate 233**
From left: sterling repoussé,
$40.00 – 50.00; sterling cut
work, circa 1875 – 1910,
$35.00 – 45.00.

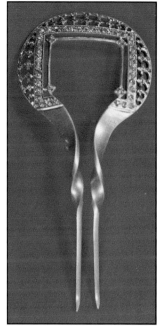

**Plate 234**
Aluminum, cut work, clear sets, circa 1870, $60.00 – 70.00.

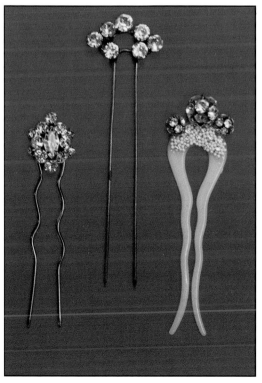

**Plate 235**
From left: steel, pastes, circa 1900, $15.00 – 20.00; steel, pastes, circa 1900, $15.00 – 20.00; celluloid, seed pearls, pastes, circa 1900, $15.00 – 20.00.

111

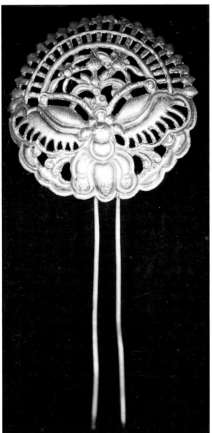

**Plate 236**
Sterling, butterfly motif, Art Nouveau, 1890 – 1910, $70.00 – 75.00.

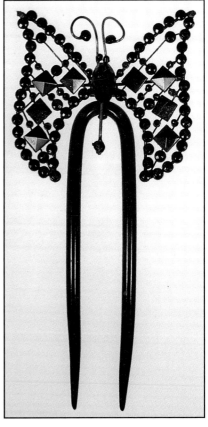

**Plate 237**
Celluloid, wire and French jet butterfly, circa 1920, $45.00 – 55.00.

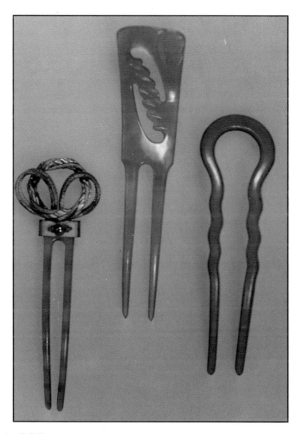

**Plate 238**

From left: horn, faux tortoise, twisted brass loops, circa 1890, $30.00 – 40.00; celluloid, open work, circa 1925, $15.00 – 20.00; celluloid, faux tortoise, circa 1870, $3.00 – 5.00.

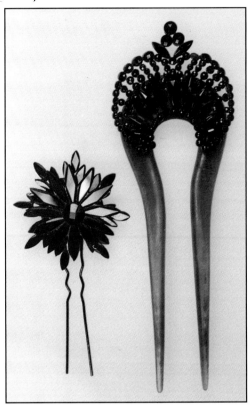

**Plate 239**

From left: wire with French jet, circa 1870 – 1890, $35.00 – 40.00; horn with French jet on wire, circa 1870, $50.00 – 60.00.

**Plate 240**

Below, from left: celluloid, seed pearls and sets, circa 1895, $15.00 – 20.00; celluloid, green pavé sets, circa 1895, $30.00 – 35.00; celluloid, clear sets, circa 1930, $30.00 – 35.00.

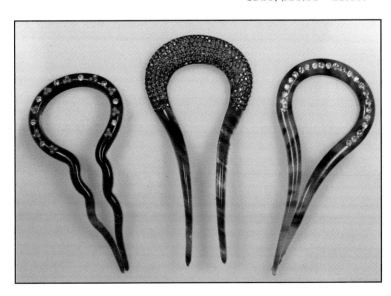

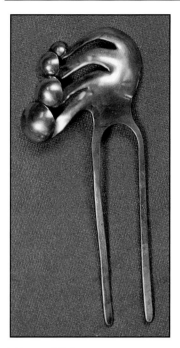

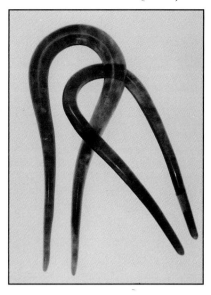

**Plate 242**
Celluloid, circa 1930, $1.00 – 3.00.

**Plate 241**
Sterling, Art Deco, 1910 –
1930, $15.00 – 20.00.

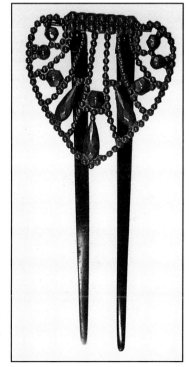

**Plate 243**
Tortoise shell, faceted
brass, hinged, circa 1850,
$20.00 – 25.00.

**Plate 244**
From left: Kingfisher, feathers on brass, $25.00 – 35.00; Kingfisher feathers, on steel, $50.00 – 60.00.

**Plate 245**
From left: Kingfisher feathers, on steel, tremblants, with butterflies, $40.00 – 50.00; Kingfisher feathers, on steel, tremblants with carnelian and seed pearls, 35.00 – 40.00.

116

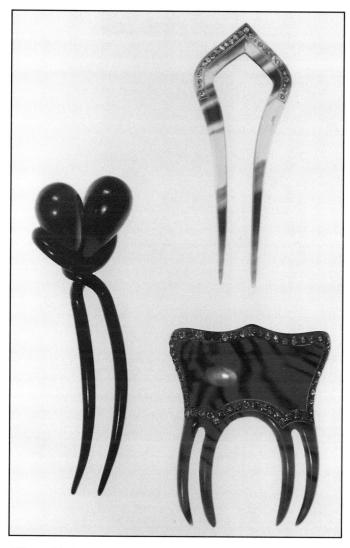

**Plate 246**

From left: celluloid, circa 1920, $15.00 – 20.00; celluloid hairpin with small sets, faux tortoise, $5.00 – 10.00; celluloid split comb, with sets, $20.00 – 25.00.

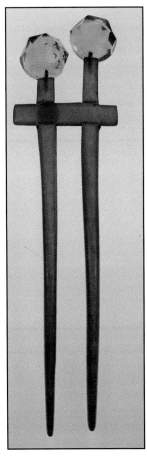

**Plate 248**
From left: Kanzasi, metal bangles and flowers, ear spoon, circa 1867 (Edo period), $100.00 – 125.00; Kansasi, tremblants with jade beads on brass, circa 1867 (Edo period), $90.00 – 100.00.

**Plate 247**
Horn with faceted glass balls, $15.00 – 20.00.

118

**Plate 249**
Bodkin, brass with plastic balls, circa 1895, $7.50 – 10.00.

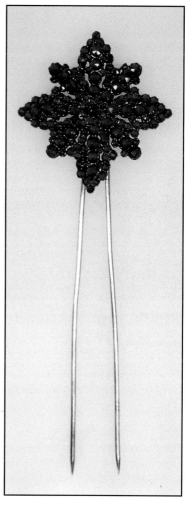

**Plate 250**
Sterling, with garnets, $150.00 – 200.00.

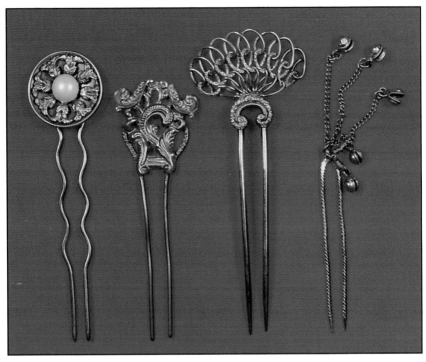

**Plate 251**
From left: steel, with pearl center, circa 1930, $25.00 – 30.00; brass, repoussé, $15.00 – 20.00; brass, $20.00 – 25.00; brass, small balls on chains, circa early 1800s, $10.00 – 15.00.

**Plate 252**
Celluloid, iridescent sets,
circa 1920, $20.00 – 25.00.

**Plate 253**
Coin silver Kan-
zasi, with ear
spoon, $35.00 –
40.00.

**Plate 254**
Brass Kanzasi,
with    coral
beads, $40.00 –
50.00.

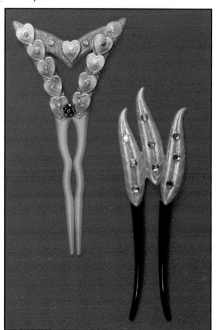

## Plate 255

From left: celluloid, steel hearts, circa 1920s, $5.00 – 7.50; celluloid, pearlized celluloid with pink sets, circa 1920s, $5.00 – 7.50.

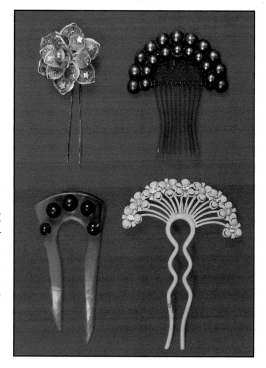

## Plate 256

Top row from left: sterling filigree (top left), $30.00 – 35.00; sterling on celluloid, $15.00 – 20.00; bottom row from left: horn, $5.00 – 7.50; steel with pink enamel, Art Nouveau, circa 1890 – 1910, $15.00 – 20.00.

**Plate 257**
Sterling, $30.00 –
40.00.

**Plate 258**
Below from left: French, celluloid,
circa 1890, 7.50 – 10.00; French, celluloid, circa 1890, $7.50 – 10.00;
French, celluloid, 1890, $7.50 – 10.00.

**Plate 259**
Tortoise shell with garnets,
hinged, circa 1830 – 1870,
$300.00 – 350.00.

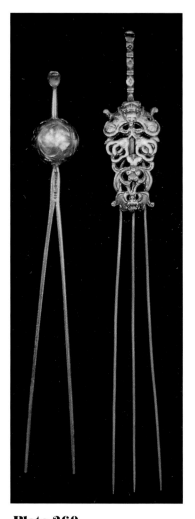

**Plate 260**
Sterling Kanzasi, etched with
ear spoon, $35.00 – 40.00;
sterling hair ornament, with
ear spoon, $35.00 – 40.00.

**Plate 261**
Celluloid with sterling,
Art Nouveau, circa 1890
– 1910, $75.00 – 80.00.

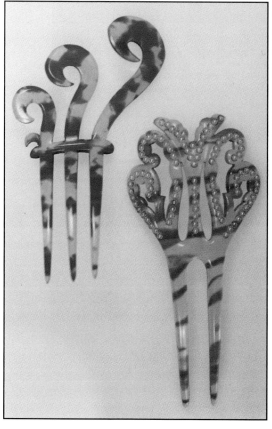

**Plate 262**
From left: faux tortoise hair ornament, celluloid, $12.00 – 15.00; faux tortoise, celluloid with seed pearls, $15.00 – 20.00.

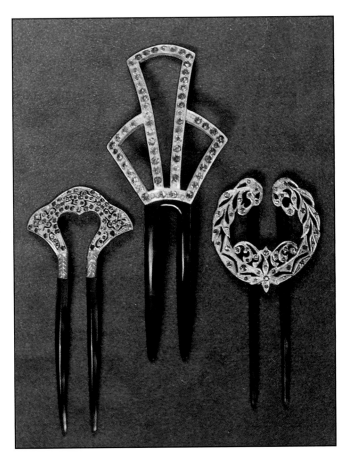

**Plate 263**
From left: celluloid with aluminum top with marcasites, $20.00 – 25.00; celluloid with aluminum top with clear sets, $35.00 – 45.00; celluloid with hinged aluminum top with clear sets, $30.00 – 40.00.

### Plate 264

Mother of pearl with gilt brass filigree, circa 1890, $35.00 – 45.00; mother of pearl with gilt brass filigree, circa 1890, $35.00 – 45.00.

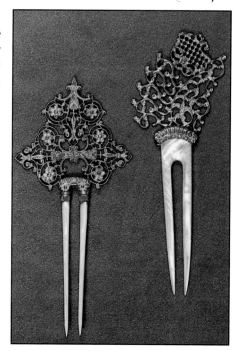

### Plate 265

Below: celluloid  brass leaves with sets, $10.00 – 12.00; celluloid, gilt brass, $10.00 – 12.00; celluloid, gilt brass, $15.00 – 20.00.

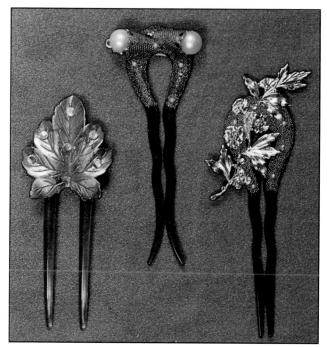

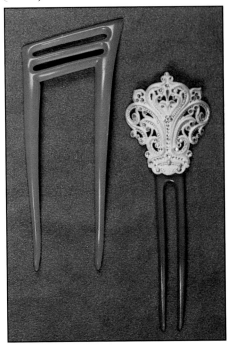

**Plate 266**

From left: amber colored celluloid, Art Deco, circa 1920, $15.00 – 20.00; horn, repoussé aluminum top, circa 1870, original box, $20.00 – 25.00.

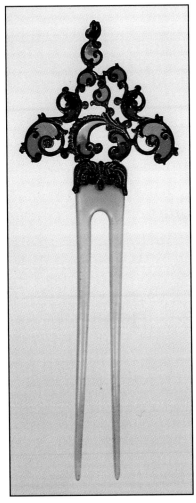

**Plate 267**

Horn with filigree and colored enamels, Art Deco, 1920s, $30.00 – 35.00.

# Hairpins

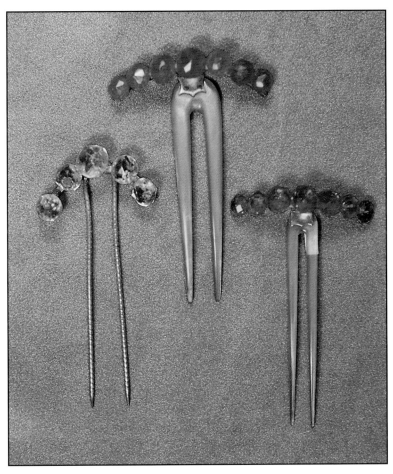

**Plate 268**
From left: brass with light amber glass balls, circa 1880, $15.00 –
20.00; horn, real amber faceted balls, circa 1880, $25.00 – 35.00;
horn, real amber faceted balls, circa 1880, $25.00 – 35.00.

129

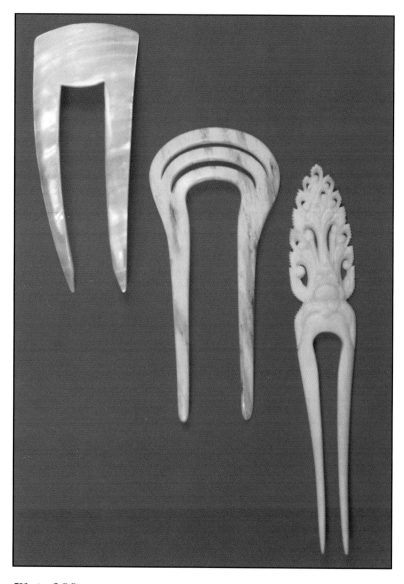

**Plate 269**
From left: mother of pearl, circa 1920s, $10.00 – 15.00; celluloid,
Art Deco, 1920s, $10.00 – 15.00; bone, $10.00 – 15.00.

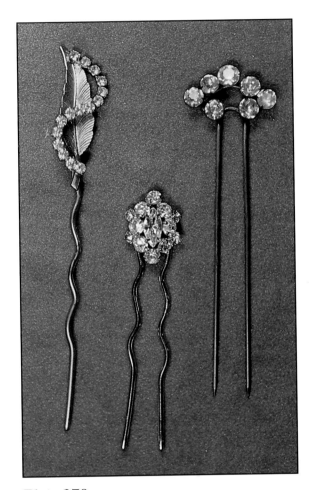

**Plate 270**
From left: steel bodkin, leaf design with pastes, circa 1895 – 1905, $10.00 – 15.00; steel hairpin with pastes, circa 1895 – 1905, $15.00 – 20.00; brass hairpin with pastes, circa 1895 – 1905, $15.00 – 20.00.

**Plate 271**

From left: celluloid, sets, circa 1910, $3.00 – 5.00; celluloid, fine brass wire meshed, circa 1900, $3.00 – 5.00; celluloid, painted design, $3.00 – 5.00.

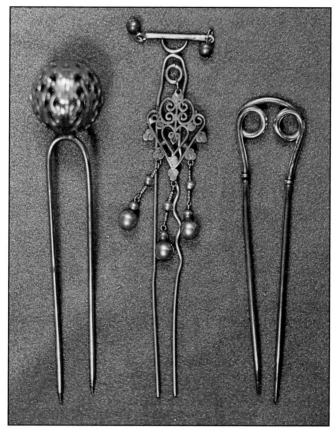

**Plate 272**

From left: rolled gold-plated, circa 1830, $20.00 – 30.00; 14K gold with bangles, circa 1810, $45.00 – 65.00; rolled gold plated, circa 1895, $20.00 – 30.00.

**Plate 273**
Silver plate, Oriental, with monkey
and grapes, $35.00 – 45.00.

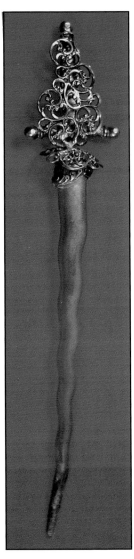

**Plate 274**
Horn bodkin with ster-
ling filigree top, circa
1895, $30.00 – 35.00.

**Plate 275**
From left: celluloid bodkin, circa 1895, $20.00 –
25.00; celluloid bodkin, circa 1895, $25.00 – 35.00;
celluloid bodkin, circa 1895, $35.00 – 40.00; cellu-
loid bodkin, circa 1895, $20.00 – 35.00.

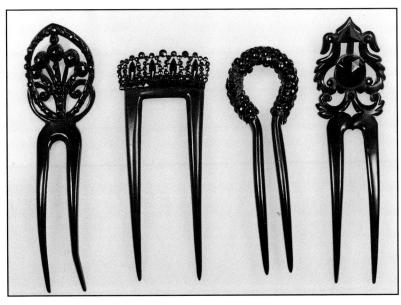

**Plate 276**
From left: celluloid with French jet, circa 1890, $20.00 – 25.00; celluloid with French jet on wire, circa 1890, $30.00 – 35.00; celluloid with French jet, circa 1890, $10.00 – 12.00; celluloid with French jet, circa 1890, $15.00 – 20.00.

**Plate 277**

From left: celluloid with clear sets, circa 1890, $5.00 –
7.50; celluloid with clear sets, circa 1890, $5.00 – 7.50;
celluloid with pastes, $5.00 – 7.50.

**Plate 278**
Sterling with stamped
designs, twentieth century,
$15.00 – 20.00.

**Plate 279**
Horn with sterling top, lily of
the valley design, Art Nouveau, $75.00 – 100.00.

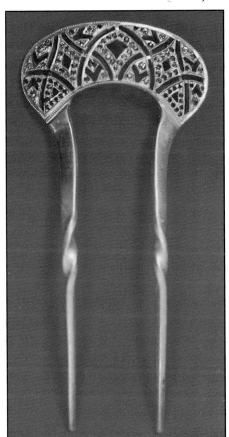

**Plate 280**
Aluminum with marcasites,
circa 1870, $50.00 – 75.00.

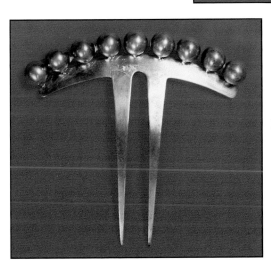

**Plate 281**
Sterling, $35.00 – 40.00.

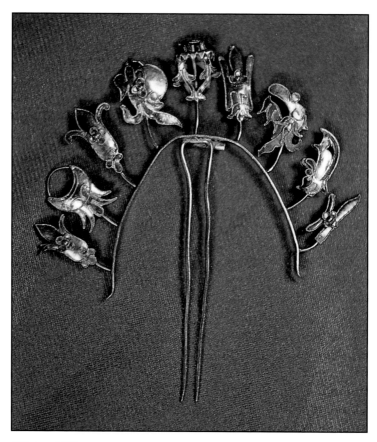

**Plate 282**
Sterling, Oriental, $40.00 – 45.00.

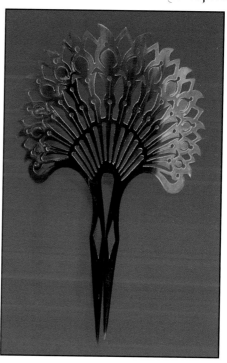

**Plate 283**
Joba or buffalo horn, cut work, circa
1885 – 1901, $25.00 – 30.00.

**Plate 284**
Tortoise shell, cut work, circa
1850, $35.00 – 40.00.

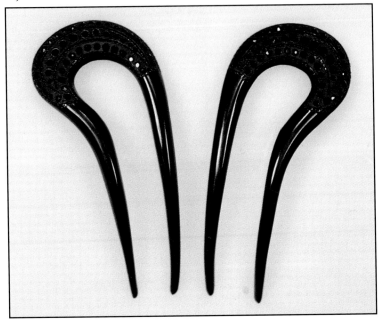

**Plate 285**
Celluloid hairpin inscribed non-inflammable, Art Deco, pair,
$70.00.

### Antique Comb Collectors Club International

The Antique Comb Collectors Club International (ACCCI) was started in Tarpon Springs, Florida, in 1993, where we held our first convention. Since then we have held a convention in 1995, in Leominster, Massachusetts, which was considered the comb capital of the world. The 1997 convention was held in the Elk Grove, Illinois, where I was elected president of the club. Our first president was Betty Miller of Homer, Alaska, who has a comb museum with nearly 4,000 decorative combs of the past. Glenn Beall, our second president, was recently honored by being inducted into the Plastics Hall of Fame. Several other members are also experts in their field and are writing books after much research, so that it will be easier for collectors in the future to garner information.

Club members are from the United States, Canada, Great Britain, the Netherlands, Belgium, and France. Through our bimonthly newsletter, written by Belva Green of Florida, we are gaining more information about our collections, learning to identify them, and find their place in history, and learning how to preserve our combs. A roster of members gives us the chance to communicate with others who are interested in collecting the beautiful combs that were worn by our ancestors. Information about the club can be obtained by writing to me, Mary Bachman, 4901 Grandview, Ypsilanti, MI 48197-3762.

# Bibliography

Boman, Ann. "French Ivory." *Martha Stewart Living*, September, 1996.

Bovin, Murray. *Jewelry Making*. Forest Hills, New York: Murray Bovin.

Clifford, Anne. *Cut Steel & Berlin Iron Jewelry*. 1971.

Doyle, Bernard W. *Comb Making in America*. Privately printed, 1925.

*Encyclopedia Brittanica*.

Fisher, F. J. *The Worshipful Company of Horners (A Short History)*. Geo. B. Cotton & Co. Ltd at the Galleon Press Cordon.

Godemberg, Rose Leiman. *All About Jewelry*. Arbor House Publishing Company and in Canada by Fitzhenry & Whiteside, Ltd., 1983.

Green, Belva. *The Antique Comb Collector's Companion*. Privately printed, 1993.

Haertig, Evelyn. *Antique Combs and Purses*. Carmel, California: Gallery Graphics Press.

Meikle, Jeffery I. *American Plastic: A Cultural History*. New Brunswick, New Jersey: Rutgers University Press, 1995.

Sutton-Smith, Barbara. "Tortoise Shell." *Antique Showcase*. July/August, 1996.

Yarwood, Doreen. *European Costume*. Great Britain: B.T. Batsford Ltd.

# Schroeder's
# ANTIQUES
## Price Guide ... is the #1 best-selling
antiques & collectibles value guide on the market today,
and here's why . . .

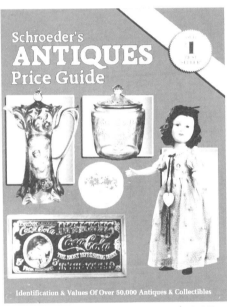